Experts on child reading levels
have consulted on the level of text and
concepts in this book.

At the end of the book is a "Look Back and Find" section
which provides additional information and encourages
the child to refer back to previous pages
for the answers to the questions posed.

Angela Grunsell trained as a teacher in 1969.
She has a Diploma in Reading and Related Skills
and for the last five years has advised London
teachers on materials and resources.

Published in the United States in 1983 by
Franklin Watts, 387 Park Avenue South, New York, NY 10016

© Aladdin Books Ltd/Franklin Watts

Designed and produced by
Aladdin Books Ltd, 70 Old Compton Street, London W1

ISBN 0 531 04718 0

Library of Congress Number:
83-50922

Printed in Belgium

FRANKLIN · WATTS · FIRST · LIBRARY

Baby Animals

Consultant
Angela Grunsell

Illustrated by
Aline Riquier and Elsa Godfrey

Franklin Watts
New York · London · Toronto · Sydney

Have you noticed how baby animals grow and change? Once you were a baby. Now you are growing and changing too.

You visit the farmer and find him at work.
The bouncy young lambs are playing together.
Their big woolly mothers look sleepy and fat.

8

Back at the farmhouse the mother sheepdog rests.

She watches you play with her puppies.

Soon they must learn to look after the sheep.

What will you do when you're grown up?

10

Inside the farmhouse is a motherless lamb.
The farmer's wife gives you a bottle of milk
and shows you how to feed him.
He nestles in your arms and drinks thirstily.

The lamb is soft and warm to hold. You think you would like him as a pet. But what would a full-grown sheep do in the house?
He must join the other sheep in the field.

13

In the farmyard a mother goose hisses.
It is a warning to stay away from her.
Her baby geese follow in a line behind her.

15

Baby chicks peck at food on the ground.

If you go too close the mother hen gets angry.
She lifts her wings and the chicks run
to hide under them.

In the pig sty the big sow lies on her side.
She grunts as the piglets feed from her.
How many piglets can you see?

A new-born calf stands in the cow-shed.
Her legs are very weak and wobbly.

An older calf has learned to drink
from a bucket.
Her legs are strong and steady now.

Horses are outside in the paddock.
The young horse is called a foal.
His nose is soft as he nuzzles your hand.

The foal runs back to his mother to feed.

He drinks only milk at the moment.

When he is older he will eat grass and hay.

These kittens are now old enough to leave their mother. Dad says you may take one home. The farmer leaves you to go back to his work.

You say goodbye to the lambs in the field.
The kitten will make a much better pet.
You will be able to watch her change and grow.

Now you must learn to look after her properly.

Look back and find

What work do sheepdogs do?

How many puppies does the sheepdog have?

How many human babies are
usually born at one time?

When do lambs need to be fed from bottles?

How do most baby lambs feed?
They feed from their mothers.

Can you find another animal that feeds
her young in the book?

How are baby geese and chicks born?
*The mother lays eggs which hatch out
into baby birds.*

What are baby geese called?
They are called goslings.

What does the mother hen do if you
go too close?

What do baby chicks feed on?
They feed on grain.

At what age can kittens leave their mothers?
They should be at least 8 weeks old.

What colors are the cats and kittens
in the picture?

Do you have a pet?

How old do you think the girl
in the story is? How old are you?

Have you seen a photograph of what
you looked like when you were a baby?

How have you changed?

Index

C   calf 20, 21
     chicks 16, 17, 28, 29

F   farmer 7, 25
     farmhouse 9, 11
     farmyard 14
     foal 22, 23

G   goose 14, 28
     goslings 28

H   hen 17, 29
     horses 22

K   kittens 25, 26, 29

L   lambs 7, 11, 12, 26, 28

P   pig 19
     piglets 19
     pig sty 19

S   sheep 9, 12
     sheepdog 9, 28
     sow 19

PRINTED IN BELGIUM BY

proost

INTERNATIONAL BOOK PRODUCTION